EARTHQUAKES

Please visit our web site at: **www.garethstevens.com**
For a free color catalog describing Gareth Stevens Publishing's list of high-quality books and multimedia programs, call **1-800-542-2595 (USA)** or **1-800-387-3178 (Canada)**. Gareth Stevens Publishing's fax: **(414) 332-3567.**

Library of Congress Cataloging-in-Publication Data

Shake.
   Earthquakes.
      p. cm. — (Discovery Channel school science: our planet Earth)
   Originally published: Shake. Bethesda, Md.: Discovery Enterprises. © 2000.
   Summary: Provides a variety of information on earthquakes including how they are measured, where they are expected to occur, how scientists study them, and some specific earthquakes in history.
     ISBN 0-8368-3378-3 (lib. bdg.)
     1. Earthquakes—Juvenile literature. [1. Earthquakes.] I. Title. II. Series.
QE521.3.S537 2004
551.22—dc22

2003059209

This edition first published in 2004 by
Gareth Stevens Publishing
A World Almanac Education Group Company
330 West Olive Street, Suite 100
Milwaukee, WI 53212 USA

This U.S. edition copyright © 2004 by Gareth Stevens, Inc. First published in 2000 as *Shake: The Earthquake Files* by Discovery Enterprises, LLC, Bethesda, Maryland. © 2000 by Discovery Communications, Inc.

Further resources for students and educators available at www.discoveryschool.com

Designed by Bill SMITH STUDIO
Creative Director: Ron Leighton
Designers: Sonia Gauba, Eric Hoffsten, Dmitri Kushnirsky, Bill Wilson, Jay Jaffe, Scott Russo
Photo Editors: Jennifer Friel, Scott Haag
Intern: Chris Pascarella
Art Buyers: Paula Radding, Rae Grant

Gareth Stevens Editor: Betsy Rasmussen
Gareth Stevens Art Director: Tammy Gruenewald
Technical Advisor: Emily Watson

Printed in the United States of America

1 2 3 4 5 6 7 8 9 08 07 06 05 04

Writers: Jackie Ball, Justine Ciovacco, Margaret Carruthers, Bonny Fetterman, Scott Ingram, Uechi Ng, Monique Peterson, Anna Prokos, Denise Vega.

Editor: Justine Ciovacco.

Photographs: Cover, Golden Gate Bridge, © Co   Stone; p. 2, 4–5, Turkey earthquake, Reuters/   Photos; pp. 3, 22, A. Cetinol, © Associated P   seismologist, © Michael Salas/Image Bank; Turkey, © AFP/CORBIS; pp. 14–15, fault line, Balog/Stone; p. 16, Great Tokyo Fire, © CORI   Tangshan, © UPI/CORBIS-Bettmann; p. 17, N   © Nick Wheeler/CORBIS; Japan '95, © Eye U CORBIS; pp. 16–17, Great Tokyo Fire, © Arch

skeleton, courtesy Madrid Library, MO; p. 20, seismologist, © Roger Ressmeyer/CORBIS; p. 21, soil layers, U.S. Dept. of the Interior/National Parks Service; Altadena, CA, courtesy Charles M. Rubin, Professor & Chair/Department of Geological Sciences/Southern California Earthquake Center/Central Washington University; p. 22, I. Cimin, © ABC AJANS/Liaison International; p. 23, Sun Chi-kwang, © Associated Press, AP; pp. 24–25, ©Virginia Task Force One/Craig Luke; p. 28, Inge Lehmann, courtesy Kort & Matrikelstyrelsen/National Survey and Cadastre, Denmark; Aristotle, © Granger Collection, New York; p. 31,   tick Park, © Lawrence Burr/Liaison Agency; All other   © Corel.

   ion: p. 13, force diagram, Phil Howe.

Earthquakes are earth shattering. Literally. Caused by the slipping and rubbing of huge rock slabs underground, earthquakes—as anyone who keeps up with the news or lives in a quake-prone area knows—are unpredictable and sometimes cause major damage.

Every year, Earth has about one million quakes. Humans can feel only about 6 percent of these. So how do we know the others happen? How have people learned to adapt to earthquakes? What has been the impact of technology on predicting quakes? Can these earth-shaking activities have a positive side? Find out about the ups and downs and ins and outs of earthquakes in Discovery Channel's EARTHQUAKES.

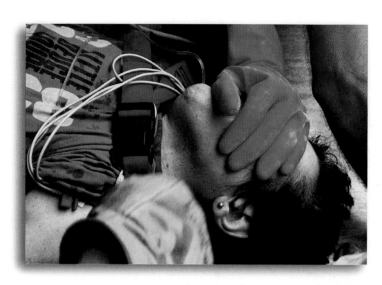

Rescue workers save a quake victim.
See page 22.

Final Project

Earthquakes

At 3:01 on the morning of August 17, 1999, people living in Izmit, Turkey, were awakened by a terrible fright. An earthquake rocked the area. It registered 7.4 on the Richter scale, which measures quake strength on a scale of 1 to 9 with 9 being the strongest. By the time the quake and its aftershocks—quakes that strike after the first quake—finished, 17,000 people were dead. More than 120,000 houses were demolished (see background picture), and the roads and railroad system were destroyed.

Quakes, also called temblors, are fairly common in that part of Turkey, but not all of them are equally destructive. Just three months later, on November 12, and 62 miles (100 kilometers) to the east, a quake measuring 7.2 hit Duzce, Turkey. This temblor was similar in intensity to the Izmit quake, but its end result was significantly less destructive. At least 700 people were killed, and more than 675 buildings collapsed.

Interestingly, both quakes struck in different places along the same fault line, or fracture in Earth's crust. Like most earthquakes, these two were caused by a sudden release of pressure along a fault line. The release shifted adjacent blocks of rock under the surface, called tectonic plates, past each other. As a result, waves of energy pushed the land both under and above ground.

The difference between the two Turkish quakes is where they struck. The exact location of a quake's epicenter—the point on Earth's surface directly above a quake's underground beginning—has a major effect on the damage an earthquake causes. The Izmit quake was centered in an industrial city filled with concrete buildings. The Duzce quake struck a hilly, farming region, which had fewer buildings and people.

Predictions of where and when an earthquake will strike are impossible to make. There is still a lot of mystery that surrounds the invisible waves that begin underground and force changes on Earth's surface. With each quake, scientists move closer to understanding these earthshaking events.

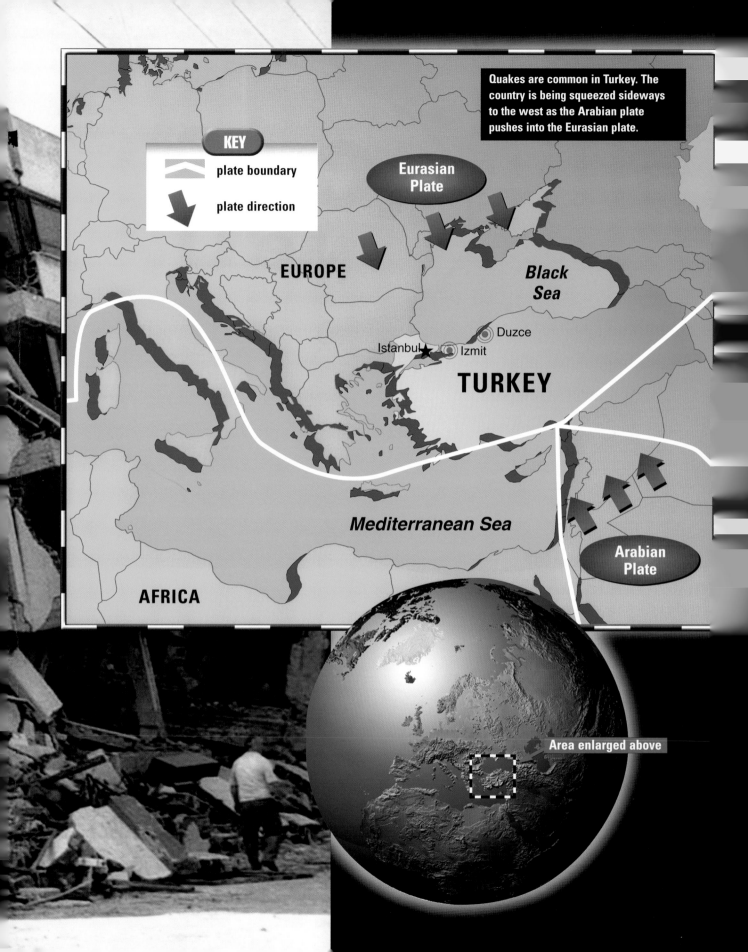

Quakes are common in Turkey. The country is being squeezed sideways to the west as the Arabian plate pushes into the Eurasian plate.

KEY

plate boundary

plate direction

Eurasian Plate

EUROPE

Black Sea

Duzce

Istanbul   Izmit

TURKEY

Mediterranean Sea

AFRICA

Arabian Plate

Area enlarged above

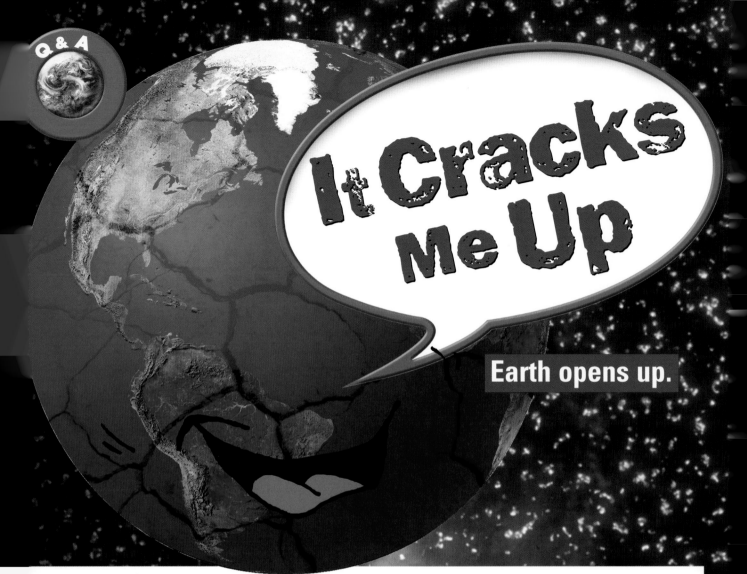

It Cracks Me Up

Earth opens up.

Q: You're Earth. Glad we finally caught up with you. You certainly keep moving.

A: Yeah, well, between my orbiting and all the other pressures of the job, sometimes I feel like I'm running in circles.

Q: Lots of pressure being a planet, eh?

A: I can't speak for the other eight, but there's a lot of pressure being this particular planet. From my iron core to my rocky crust, I'm nothing but a big ball of heat and pressure. Sometimes I think I'm going to crack, but then I remember that's not possible because I'm already cracked!

Q: What?

A: Well, my crust has been broken into huge slabs, called tectonic plates, for as long as I can remember. And I have a long memory—more than four billion years. The cracking happened as my surface cooled off, after I was formed. You're standing on one right now. But don't worry—all plates are at least 43 miles (69 km) thick.

Q: You've got a reputation for being so together. I'm puzzled as to how you could be in pieces.

A: Just goes to show that you can't believe everything you see or hear. I look solid because those slabs fit together so nicely. Well, except that they are moving.

Q: Moving? Are you sure? I don't feel anything.

A: They're not moving very fast. Actually, your hair grows about six times as fast as my plates move. But the plates drift along on the melted rock that makes up most of my mantle, which is the next layer down from the crust.

Q: But if these plates are drifting, how do they all stay together?

A: That's the problem: They don't. They push together, pull apart, and slide past each other. Because they're so huge—some are big enough to hold whole continents—their movement makes massive amounts of tension in the rocks deep inside me. The rocks stretch and bend to absorb the strain, but all of a sudden, I can't stand it and I snap. I release the tension all at once as vibrations. Invisible waves of energy come rolling out in all directions. When they reach the surface, you've got yourself an earthquake. And I feel so much calmer. But before you know it, the tension begins to mount again.

Q: **Sounds like it could be tough on you. How often does this happen?**

A: Oh, I lose count after awhile. But scientists keep track on the surface, and some of them say earthquakes happen almost every second.

Q: **Wait a minute. We only hear about earthquakes once in awhile.**

A: That's because most earthquakes never make the news. They're tiny tremors. You hear about the big ones that cause a lot of damage and destruction. And I take full responsibility. It's all my fault. Make that, all my faults.

Q: **What do you mean?**

A: Faults are weak places in my crust where earthquakes are likeliest to surface—where all that pent-up energy down below tries to escape. You'll find them mostly around the edges of my plates. I've got hundreds of thousands of faults. But hey, nobody's perfect.

Q: **What do faults look like?**

A: That depends. Those big jigsaw pieces of tectonic plates move in different ways, and that affects the kind of force the rocks in my crust have to absorb. And that affects how a fault looks.

Q: **Can you give me an example?**

A: Sure. I'll give you three. Some plates move away from each other. They're called divergent plates. That kind of movement can wrench rocks apart. So rocks around the fault line are pushed down, creating valleys such as California's Death Valley. Mountain ridges can be formed on either side of this fault, which is called a normal fault. This type of movement can cause violent earthquakes.

Q: **What's another example?**

A: It's called a reverse fault. It happens at the edges of plates that are moving toward each other, called convergent plates. The plates collide and rocks above the fault surface are pushed over the rocks on the other side. Pieces of crust pile up on each other and form mountains.

Q: **You said there were three.**

A: Yup, the third type are strike-slip faults. One of my favorites, California's San Andreas Fault, is that kind. Strike-slip faults happen in places where plates slide by each other in opposite directions. Pretend you're running down a very narrow hallway on your way to class. Someone else is running toward you. You scrape shoulders as you run past each other, and one or both of you get knocked sideways. That's why strike-slip faults make the earth move horizontally. These happen a lot but tend to be less dramatic. You know, no matter the type of fault, all earthquakes are about energy—built-up energy released as vibrations that move in waves up and out of the rocks in my crust. They're as natural for me as breathing is for you.

Q: **Well, natural or not, don't you wish you didn't have such a destructive side to you?**

A: But earthquakes aren't all destructive. Sometimes they're constructive. In other words, they don't just destroy land—they create it, too.

Q: **How? Where?**

A: Under the ocean, earthquakes can make cracks in the ocean floor, where my crust is very thin. Hot magma comes seeping up, gets cooled by the water, and hardens. And you have brand-new land! In fact, scientists know now what I've known all my life: Earth's crust is being created and destroyed at the same rate. And earthquakes have a lot to do with keeping that in balance.

Q: **And volcanoes, too.**

A: Sure, but that's another book. I've got to get going. I'm feeling a little tense, and you never know when I'm going to snap!

Activity

MODEL BEHAVIOR Boil an egg and crack the shell. Notice that the shell is not sitting tightly on the cooked egg. What do the shell pieces have in common with Earth's plates? If you squeeze the egg gently between two fingers, what happens? What does this represent? How can you make different shell pieces move in different directions (as Earth's plates do)?

Sizing Up the Seismos

When reading about earthquakes, you will see the term "seismo" a lot. That prefix comes from the Greek word "seismos," which means earthquakes. Scientists who study earthquakes are called seismologists.

For Good Measure

A seismologist holds a sample reading from a seismograph.

Seismologists measure the location and strength of quake vibrations using a seismograph. A seismograph's main parts are a cylinder with paper around it, a spring, a weight, and a pen. One end of the spring is attached to at least one pole in the ground, while the other end has the weight with a pen stuck to it. The paper around the cylinder presses against the pen, turning and constantly recording earthquake-caused invisible wave motions in Earth. Everything in the seismograph moves except the weight and its attached pen. The pen draws jagged lines—called a seismogram—on the shaking paper, creating a record of ground activity. The more jagged the line, the more intense the vibrations. Read more about seismograms on page 13.

A seismogram won't tell seismologists precisely where a quake's epicenter was, but it can show how many miles or kilometers away from the seismograph the earthquake occurred. When looking for an epicenter, seismologists must have the recordings from at least two other seismographs in another part of the world to pinpoint the quake's exact location.

Quake by Numbers

The Richter scale, invented in 1935 by seismologists Charles F. Richter and Beno Gutenberg, measures quake magnitude or strength on a numerical scale. The bigger the number, the more powerful the quake. On the Richter scale, each step up in magnitude (from 4.0 to 5.0, for example) uses 30 times more energy than the one below it. People barely feel a 2.0, while a 6.0 or higher magnitude quake is considered substantial.

Check this chart to find out how many earthquakes the world experiences at different magnitudes on the Richter scale.

Magnitude	Description	Occurrences per year (unless otherwise noted)
1.0 – 1.9	Extremely minor	About 8,000 per day
2.0 – 2.9	Very minor	About 1,000 per day
3.0 – 3.9	Minor	Approximately 49,000
4.0 – 4.9	Light	Approximately 6,200
5.0 – 5.9	Moderate	800
6.0 – 6.9	Strong	120
7.0 – 7.9	Major	18
8.0 and higher	Great	1

Tale of Another Scale

Italian seismologist Giuseppe Mercalli created the Mercalli scale in 1902. Unlike the Richter scale, his scale noted the observed effects of an earthquake on people and property. In 1931, American seismologists Harry Wood and Frank Neumann developed the Modified Mercalli scale, which is currently used in the United States. The Modified Mercalli scale describes the strength or intensity of underground movements. Instead of using scientific measurements like a seismograph, the Mercalli scale uses twelve sensory observations to explain intensity.

The Modified Mercalli scale is shown below. This scale uses Roman numerals for its levels. These numbers do not correspond with the numbers used in the Richter scale.

A quake in Turkey rocked this home off its foundation.

Modified Mercalli scale	What happens?
I	Most people don't notice.
II	Hanging objects may sway.
III	People indoors will feel movement but may not recognize as quake.
IV	Felt indoors, some dishes and windows disturbed, walls may crack.
V	Felt by most, dishes and windows break, unstable objects overturned.
VI	Felt by all, heavy furniture moves, plaster may fall.
VII	People may fall, walls may crack.
VIII	Heavy furniture falls over, some walls crumble, damage minimal to well-built structures, damage severe to poorly built structures.
IX	Heavy damage to all structures, partial collapse possible.
X	Some wooden structures destroyed, rails bent.
XI	Few, if any, masonry buildings remain standing, bridges destroyed.
XII	Total damage, objects thrown into the air.

When's It SHAKIN'?

Seismologists cannot predict precisely when an earthquake will occur, but they can provide a "forecast." They do this in two ways: by examining and recording the history of large earthquakes in specific areas, and by looking at how quickly strain on Earth's plates builds up. Seismologists can often come within a few days with their predictions.

Activity

SNAP TO IT This four-person experiment should help you understand why we need three seismographs to locate a quake's epicenter. Have three blindfolded students stand in different locations around the classroom. The fourth student should stand away from the others and snap his or her fingers. The other three should immediately point in the direction of the sound. The fourth student should map a line from where each of the three students stand to the point where they say they heard the sound. The lines should intersect at the exact location of the sound. How does this method locate the epicenter of an earthquake? Would it be possible for just one student to locate the sound? Why?

A Lot on Our Plates

KEY

▪ quakes with a magnitude 6.5 or higher in 1999

⬦ plate boundary

Juan de Fuca Plate →

NORTH AMERICA

North American Plate

Caribbean Plate ↙

Pacific Plate

Fiji Plate

Indo-Australian Plate

Cocos Plate

Nazca Plate

SOUTH AMERICA

South American Plate

Antarctic Plate

Scotia Plate

Although it doesn't look like it to us, below the surface, Earth is cracked like a hard-boiled egg's shell. Heat and energy-wave motion underground shape the layers above, particularly the crust, or outer layer. The crust is made up of numerous plates—moving sections under the surface, below continents and ocean floors—vying for space. When sections of the plates get stuck, pressure will build along a fault line. Eventually the plates manage to break free, sending energy waves through the various layers underground. The result is an earthquake.

As you can see from the map, most quakes take place near plate boundaries. Yet all faults are not along such boundaries, so quakes don't always strike in obvious places. Just ask the residents of New Madrid, Missouri (see page 18).

While almost all fault lines are marks of earthquake territory, many faults will never be detected. The majority of faults are very small and movement along them is insignificant. North America's most famous fault, the San Andreas, is located along the North American

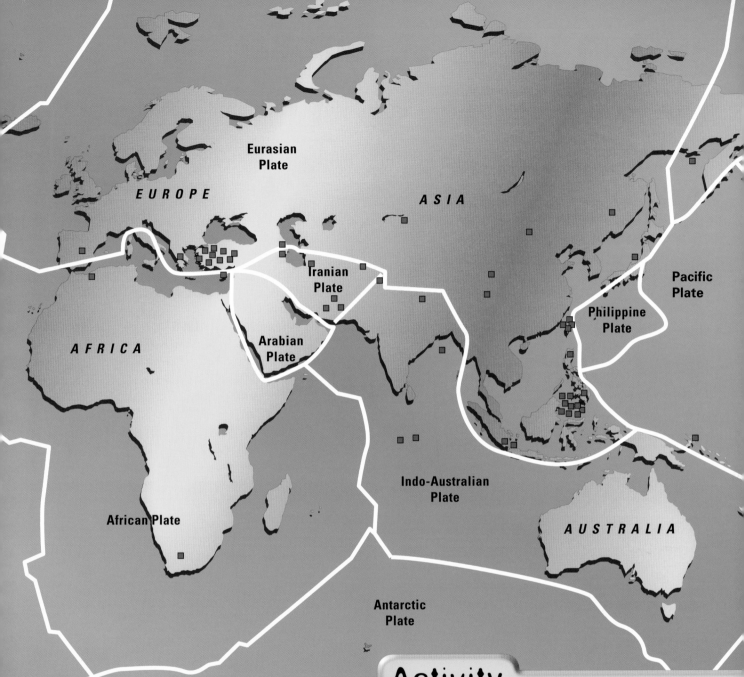

Eurasian
Plate

EUROPE

ASIA

Pacific
Plate

Iranian
Plate

Philippine
Plate

Arabian
Plate

AFRICA

Indo-Australian
Plate

AUSTRALIA

African Plate

Antarctic
Plate

and Pacific plates. It runs through San Francisco, California, making that city a prime area for quakes. On the other side of the world, the Japanese city of Tokyo similarly has a maze of underground faults.

All this activity may have you thinking that plates move fast, but that's not true. Most plates move about 1 to 2 inches (2.5 to 5 centimeters) each year. It's just that the energy they build up to move is so massive that Earth can't always take the pressure.

Activity

FIGURING OUT LAND FORMS Tectonic plates do a lot more than make Earth shake. Over millions of years, they've managed to change the landscape. Could the plates have something to do with the formation of the following landmarks: Sandia Mountains in New Mexico, Mt. Gould in Montana's Glacier National Park, Wyoming's Grand Teton Mountains, Kaibab Plateau in Arizona? Plot these spots on a map and compare their locations to where you know plates are situated. Can you name other landscapes that may have been changed by plate movement?

Wave Watch

San Francisco, April 18, 1906

This is one of the most exciting days in the life of G.K. Gilbert, a geologist working for the U.S. Geological Survey. He explains why:

It is the natural and legitimate ambition of a properly constituted geologist to see a glacier, witness an eruption, and feel an earthquake. When therefore, I was awakened in Berkeley on the 18th of April . . . by a tumult of motions and noises, it was with unalloyed pleasure that I became aware that a rigorous earthquake was in progress.

Gilbert witnessed the results of one of the most famous quakes in the United States—the San Francisco quake of 1906. From his home in Berkeley, 15 miles (24 km) east of the epicenter, he wrote the following observations about the quake in his diary.

Wednesday, April 18, 1906

An earthquake shock at 5:11 followed by others at intervals. I note [them at] 6:11 and 7:47, also 6:53 p.m. Motion in my room North-South, in other rooms East-West. Water spilled from

San Francisco

Berkeley

California

pitcher. Duration estimated at 1 minute. No apparent damage in laboratory.

Thursday, April 19, 1906

Unsuccessful attempts to go to San Francisco. A faint [after]shock at 10:15 p.m.

Friday, April 20, 1906

[travels to San Francisco] The made ground about lower Market Street shows much settling . . . [perhaps as much as] 3 to 4 feet [1 to 1.2 meters]. The buildings on this ground suffered more from earthquake than those on firm ground.

On Shaky Ground

The amount of damage energy waves can do often depends on what kind of ground they are shaking. Note Gilbert's comment about the "made" ground allowing for more damage to the structures above it. Loose soil shakes more than solid bedrock. This is why San Francisco residents should be concerned about their marina district: It was built over a landfill made by the rubble from the 1906 quake!

RIDING THE WAVES

Earthquakes happen when underground rock breaks, causing vibrations and releasing huge amounts of energy. The waves ripple through the earth, radiating out from the place where the rock broke, moving the earth up and down, forward and backward, and side to side.

Different kinds of waves travel in distinct ways and at dissimilar speeds. Body waves travel through the body of Earth. Surface waves move over Earth's surface.

There are two kinds of body waves: primary and secondary. Primary waves, called P waves, are the fastest, so they are the first ones we feel. Many people can hear P waves before they feel the rumbling and rattling. P waves move the rock forward and backward, squeezing and extending the rock.

The next waves we feel are secondary, or S waves. These waves shake the rocks up and down and from side to side. They often cause the most damage.

The Force Isn't With You

The motions you feel in an earthquake are caused by surface waves coming directly from the focus of the earthquake and body waves that have been bounced around under Earth's surface.

Whether seismic waves cause a quick jerking motion or a slow rolling motion depends on how long each wave is and how fast it moves. P and S waves create jerks and jolts because they are short and fast. Surface waves are rolling because each wave is long and slow. Even though surface waves are slower, they travel farther. Body waves die out more quickly.

Direct surface waves.

Earthquake focus: Waves travel in many directions.

Bouncing body waves.

READING RIGHT

Seismic waves can be felt around the globe. Below is a seismogram from the 1906 San Francisco earthquake. The moment it hit, this seismogram was recorded 6,100 miles (9,815 km) away in Gottingen, Germany. The captions explain each part of the seismogram.

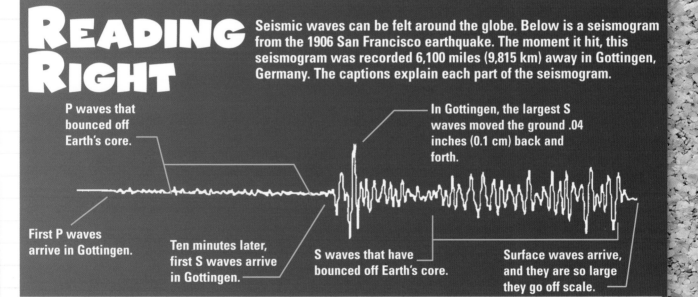

P waves that bounced off Earth's core.

In Gottingen, the largest S waves moved the ground .04 inches (0.1 cm) back and forth.

First P waves arrive in Gottingen.

Ten minutes later, first S waves arrive in Gottingen.

S waves that have bounced off Earth's core.

Surface waves arrive, and they are so large they go off scale.

Activity

MAKING WAVES Imagine that you are an earthquake creating P and S waves. You can re-create the waves, using yourself and a friend as "the quake," and a metal Slinky™ as a substitute for the wave that passes through rock. To begin, you'll need a non-carpeted floor. Sitting across from each other, you and your friend should each take an end of the Slinky. Make sure you are sitting close enough so that the Slinky isn't completely extended.

Rest the Slinky on the floor. Create a P wave: Give one end of the Slinky a quick push forward. Can you see the compressed part running down to your friend and then bouncing back? Behind the compressed part near your hand is an extended section. Notice that it is the energy wave, not the Slinky itself, that moves from you to your friend. How can you now create an S wave? Try doing so and watch the wave run down the Slinky and bounce back.

What happens when you put a piece of cardboard or wood through the middle of the Slinky and then try to make waves? What real-life earthquake experience is this similar to? When the wave gets to your end of the Slinky, you can feel it in your hand. What happens to the wave energy when it hits your hand? What does this represent?

Ride the Quakin'

You're on the San Andreas fault line, a crack in the earth that runs along California's coast. Seismologists say it's this fault's fault that earthquakes frequently hit San Francisco and its surrounding areas. Climb inside. The ride is smooth, until it gets rough. We're 10 miles (16 km) below the surface of Earth—that's where most earthquakes start.

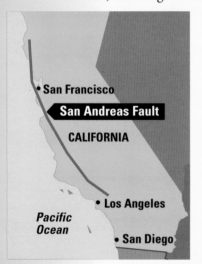

Feeling warm? You're getting close to the mantle. Another 25 miles (40 km) of this crust and Earth turns into hundreds of miles (kilometers) of molten goo before it reaches the core. Let's stay away from there.

Feel that pressure on your left and right? It's coming from the Pacific and North American tectonic plates pushing against each other. If you think that's something, just wait.

Quit pushing, Pacific! You, too, North American! These plates! Can't you just stay in one place? If one of you isn't slipping under the other, then you're sliding apart or pressing together.

Oh no! Feel that? An earthquake is coming on. Fasten your seat belt: The ride is about to start. Here we go!

Now you're riding on a P wave, and you're moving forward, rumbling back and forth, fast and furious straight through Earth.

Watch out! Up ahead is a layer of rock. **BAM!** The P wave bounces off a sturdy layer of rock and then starts heading toward the surface. How do you like this rumbling back and forth, like a roller coaster changing speed? You must be getting used to it.

BoING!

Snap!

Coaster

You're moving up, up, up—you're near the surface of Earth. **SPLASH!** Suddenly, you're no longer on a P wave. Now you're on a surface wave that moves like fast ripples in a pond (left). It's like surfing on the ground. But it's not quite as fast as the P wave.

The wave you're riding is very strong. Good thing you're in a deserted area with few people. **RUMBLE! CRASH!** You ride along the ground and it shakes and breaks. As you rip across the desert, the wave tears gashes in the soil and uproots trees. You shake the ground, and even hills, like shaking dust from a rug.

Things are beginning to slow down now. Is the ride coming to an end?

Wait! You're suddenly back at the fault line. How did that happen?

More rumbling and noise. Here we go again!

You're now on a secondary wave, an S wave. You're moving through Earth again, but this time it's a little different. Now you're rumbling side to side as you move forward, almost like a snake slithering through the grass. But this is a rougher ride, back and forth, side to side. It's shaking up the ground harder than the last wave you rode.

Ten miles (16 km), one hundred miles (161 km), one thousand miles (1,609 km) . . . **BAM!** You hit a layer of rocks and bounce back. You snake your way up to the surface. Now you're on another surface wave. **CRASH! BANG!** The ground along this wave begins to tremble. Trees shake, walls crumble. Watch out! An abandoned farmhouse splits in two.

Like the other surface wave, this one slows down, too. Eventually it stops.

Whew! Quite a ride!

Activity

FOR YOUR AMUSEMENT Now that you've "experienced" an earthquake, did it remind you of the back and forth motion of certain amusement park rides? How can you explain the differences between P waves and S waves to someone, using amusement park rides as a model? Write a description of each wave along with the appropriate ride.

Shake, Rattle, and Toll

Some of the most powerful earthquakes have not only changed landscapes, but also the lives of people who inhabit them. As you can see from this list of some of the twentieth century's most destructive quakes, a quake's magnitude does not directly relate to the damage caused.

September 1, 1923

Where: Kwanto, Japan

Magnitude: 8.3

Damage: Started Great Tokyo Fire

Lives lost: 143,000+

May 22, 1960

Where: Southern Chile

Magnitude: 8.5

Damage: $550 million to southern Chile; resulting tsunami caused $75 million damage in Hawaii, $50 million in Japan, and $500,000 on the western United States coastline

Lives lost: approximately 2,000 in Chile, 61 in Hawaii, 138 in Japan; 2 million homeless

February 9, 1971

Where: San Fernando, California, United States

Magnitude: 6.6

Damage: More than $500 million

Lives lost: 65

July 27, 1976

Where: Tangshan, China

Magnitude: 8.0

Damage: $5.6 million

Lives lost: 255,000 (with some estimates as high as 655,000); 800,000 injured

Kwanto, Japan, 1923

Tangshan, China, 1976

The GOOD NEWS About Quakes

Would you believe earthquakes can also have a positive effect on society? Over the last century, some of the world's most destructive quakes have helped provide us with valuable information. One of the areas in which this has been most striking is in the development of specific earthquake-proofing codes, which are building requirements that architects and builders must follow if they want to build in a particular area.

It wasn't until after an earthquake in Santa Barbara, California, on June 28, 1925, (6.3 magnitude, 13 deaths, $8 million in damage) that California building codes began to include specific earthquake-design provisions. It took another two years for the United States to create the first edition of the Uniform Building Code, which sets building safety standards across the country.

Other countries followed when the time was right for them. For example, Turkey did not put building codes in place until 1939, when a 7.9 magnitude quake (33,000 deaths) hit the Erzincan province.

September 19, 1985

Where: Mexico City, Mexico

Magnitude: 8.1

Damage: More than $4 billion

Lives lost: 9,500

Mexico City, Mexico, 1985

December 7, 1988

Where: Spitak, Northern Armenia

Magnitude: 6.9, four minutes later 5.8 aftershock

Damage: $14.2 billion

Lives lost: 25,000; 56 villages destroyed

June 21, 1990

Where: Manjil, Northern Iran

Magnitude: 7.7

Damage: Caused landslides; cost unknown; asked for $8.8 billion in international relief

Lives lost: 40,000; 105,000 homeless

January 17, 1995

Where: Kobe, Japan

Magnitude: 6.9

Damage: $30 to $40 billion (with estimates as high as $150 billion)

Lives lost: 6,000; 350,000 homeless

Kobe, Japan, 1995

Activity

PROTECT AND SERVE Every earthquake provides scientists with more data, which may help minimize damage during future earthquakes. Research to see if your city or town has done anything to protect against major earthquake damage. What precautions would you suggest your area take? Write a letter to your mayor explaining why your area needs more protection against earthquakes and what you think can be done. If you know that quakes are uncommon in your area, research a more seismic region's current quake-proofing activities.

AN UNCOMMON OCCURRENCE

Not all of North America's biggest quakes occur along plate boundaries. One of the most memorable series of quakes struck in the heartland of the United States—the Missouri "boot heel" and surrounding areas of Arkansas, Illinois, Kentucky, and Tennessee. The New Madrid (MAD-rid) earthquake and its aftershocks rocked this area for eight weeks (see map, right).

From December 1811 to February 1812, people in the area of the New Madrid fault felt the earth trembling almost every day. The quakes hit before the invention of the Richter scale, but scientists estimate that the most destructive quakes—which took place on December 16, January 23, and February 7—all measured 8.0 or higher. These quakes were so powerful that they were felt as far away as 600 miles (965 km) in every direction. Doors and windows rattled in New York and Washington, DC. Church bells chimed in Boston. Brick chimneys toppled in Cincinnati.

SURVIVING THE SHOCKS

On December 16, 1811, Eliza Bryan, a teacher in New Madrid, was awakened at 2 A.M. by the violent shaking of the first earthquake. She said she heard "a very awful noise, resembling loud but distant thunder." Within minutes, the air was filled with a foul-smelling "sulfurous vapor," causing total darkness.

Eliza's family fled the house to avoid falling logs and bricks and spent the rest of the night outdoors. Throughout the night, she heard "screams of the frightened inhabitants, the cries of the fowls and beasts of every species, the cracking of trees falling, and the roaring of the Mississippi [River]." When daybreak came, the sky was black with fog. Two more quakes struck at 7 A.M. and 11 A.M. For the next twelve to eighteen months, families in Eliza's area lived in temporary camps for fear of returning to their houses.

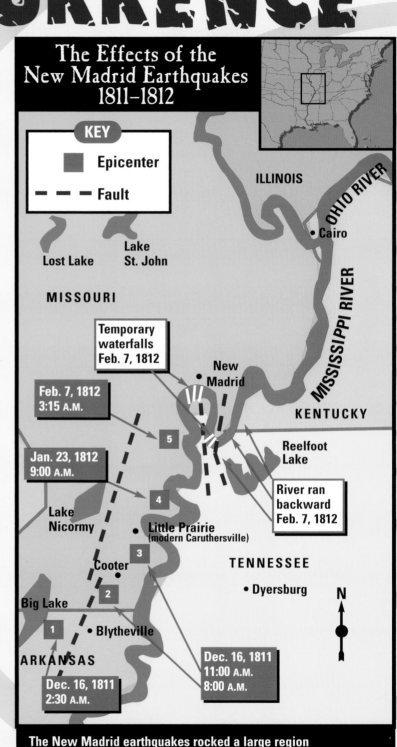

The Effects of the New Madrid Earthquakes 1811–1812

KEY

■ Epicenter

— — — Fault

ILLINOIS

OHIO RIVER

Cairo

Lost Lake

Lake St. John

MISSOURI

MISSISSIPPI RIVER

Temporary waterfalls Feb. 7, 1812

New Madrid

Feb. 7, 1812 3:15 A.M.

KENTUCKY

5

Reelfoot Lake

Jan. 23, 1812 9:00 A.M.

4

River ran backward Feb. 7, 1812

Lake Nicormy

Little Prairie (modern Caruthersville)

3

TENNESSEE

Cooter

Dyersburg

2

N

Big Lake

1

Blytheville

ARKANSAS

Dec. 16, 1811 11:00 A.M. 8:00 A.M.

Dec. 16, 1811 2:30 A.M.

The New Madrid earthquakes rocked a large region between 1811 and 1812, affecting the land in four states.

TWO TOWNS COVERED BY WATER

Little Prairie, another river town south of New Madrid, quickly became a swamp. Long, narrow trenches, called fissures, opened up across the land and filled with water, mud, and quicksand. People fled on foot in the middle of night, wading through waist-high water alongside snakes and frightened animals swimming for their lives.

According to sixteen-year-old Ben Chartier, "the earth broke open and trees fell across, so we had to 'coon the logs.'" That meant his family had to crawl over fallen trees like raccoons to cross the fissures. When they reached New Madrid, they found that the settlers had also abandoned their houses.

New Madrid resident Louis Bringier said that gases from the ground "rushed out in all quarters," spraying up dust from coal and wood in geysers of 10 to 15 feet (3 to 5 m) that "fell in a black shower." All the while, he added, "the roaring and whistling of the air escaping seemed to increase the horrible disorder of the trees [which were] cracking and splitting and falling by thousands at a time."

NOT ON SOLID GROUND

George Crist was desperate to leave New Madrid after his daughter was killed by a falling log. "If we do not get away from here," he wrote at the time, "the ground is going to eat us alive. We had another one of them earthquakes yesterday and today the ground still shakes at times. We are all about to go crazy from pain and fright."

John James Audubon, a painter and naturalist, was riding his horse when one quake struck. He saw "a sudden and strange darkness rising from the western horizon" and heard what sounded like "the distant rumbling of a violent tornado." His horse was too scared to move. Then he noticed that "the ground rose and fell in successive furrows like the ruffled waters of a lake." What he was seeing were seismic waves rippling over the surface of the land.

The quakes opened cracks in the ground that cut across this skeleton buried in Cooter, Missouri.

AN ALTERED LAND

The February 7 quake sank islands in the Mississippi River. Captain Paul Sarpy had tied his boat to Island #94 when his scouts told him that there were river pirates on it. He decided to move his boat farther downstream. By daybreak, he noted that both the island and its pirates had disappeared. Another captain reported that parts of the Mississippi ran backward—from south to north—for several hours.

The quakes made many permanent changes in the landscape. Lakes, such as Tennessee's Reelfoot Lake, were formed as the land sank and filled with water. Forests were covered with water.

During the quakes, gases spewed up from the cracked earth along with sand and water. Today, the New Madrid landscape is still marked with "sand blows," craterlike pits filled with sand.

Many parts of five towns, including New Madrid and Little Prairie, eventually sank below the Mississippi River. Although the area was sparsely populated, it is estimated that as many as one thousand people died as a result of the quakes, including traders who camped outside the villages, Native Americans in settlements along the riverbanks, and those who perished in boats and canoes.

The New Madrid fault lines extend from present-day Blytheville, Arkansas, to Cairo, Illinois. A quake as strong as the New Madrid earthquakes of 1811–1812 would be much more devastating today because there are cities along the Mississippi with millions of people, tall buildings, gas and electric lines, water mains, bridges, and highways.

Activity

LOCATOR MAP Draw the New Madrid fault line on a map of the U.S. Then write an editorial about how a future quake could affect specific regions. Would you expect Churchill Downs in Kentucky to be affected? What damage might Chicago expect? How might Nashville be affected? What about the St. Louis Arch?

Get a Clue

Tectonic forces have been creating earthquakes for millions of years. But how can scientists learn about historical quakes without written records? They search buildings, structures, and land for evidence. Often, what they find provides clues to Earth's movements—past and future.

Buried Evidence Beneath Athens, Greece, lies an entire city buried by centuries of devastating earthquakes. Archaeologists have been unearthing ancient ruins for decades. What they've found—from cooking utensils to cemeteries—shows the city's violent quaking past. By studying how structures have been buried or damaged, scientists estimate that Athens's quake history dates as far back as 300 to 400 B.C. They believe a quake in 426 B.C. shook Athens, damaging the northeast corner of its famous temple, the Parthenon (above).

Seismologist Susanna Falsaperla studies a seismograph.

Lake Quake Could the depths of Lake Tahoe (right), which straddles the border of Nevada and California, provide evidence to past earthquakes? Some scientists think so. Steve Wesnousky, director of the University of Nevada at Reno's Center for Neotectonic Studies, searched sediments from the lake's floor. He found that the sediments appear to have been folded—possibly by earthquakes. Soil samples from the lake bed also reveal evidence of a massive landslide across the lake's middle. Scientists are still researching the area to learn if the landslide was also triggered by a quake.

Marked in the Mud

On January 26, 1700, at 9 P.M., the ground *dropped off* the coasts of Washington State and Oregon. What happened? A quake with a magnitude of about 9.0 rocked the area. This quake was a subduction zone quake, which means it occurred when the ground dropped straight down, causing tsunamis (sue-NA-mees)—monstrous waves triggered by quakes under the seafloor. Scientists found that the Pacific plate, along the western coast of the United States, slipped, dropping the ground and stirring up tsunamis.

The soil and surrounding vegetation of Willapa Bay in Washington tells the story of a devastating quake and tsunami. By studying the land, scientists hypothesized that soil and sand layers now deep underground (right) could only have been deposited by tsunamis. The tsunamis were also responsible for burying entire forests of red cedar there. How do we

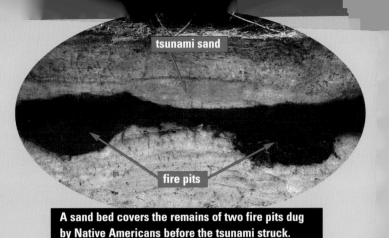

tsunami sand

fire pits

A sand bed covers the remains of two fire pits dug by Native Americans before the tsunami struck.

know? Scientists studying buried trees found that the last year the trees grew a ring in their trunks was in 1699. This supports the belief that a quake struck Washington in 1700. Japan's historical records also provide evidence of it: A tsunami washed onto the Japanese island of Honshu on January 27, 1700.

King-size Quake

Greece's island of Crete is known for its ancient quake sites. The rubble pile, bulging walls, and shaky foundation of the Palace of Knossos (above), first built around 1400 B.C., gives clues to past quakes. Seismologists believe that Crete has suffered about three major earthquakes each century. Around 1720 B.C., the famous palace was struck and damaged by a massive earthquake. The palace was rebuilt—only to be destroyed again by another quake. Stones near the palace have been knocked out of place. Scientists believe that is the result of tsunamis pulling the stones toward the ocean after a quake.

The dig site in Altadena.

Digging up Dirt

There is a lot of evidence of recent quakes in California, but in July 1999, a team of geologists started searching for clues to past quakes. The team dug 18 feet (5 m) underground in the town of Altadena. The scientists learned that two quakes, one of 7.2 magnitude and the other of 7.6, struck 12 miles (19 km) from downtown Los Angeles about 10,000 years ago. How did they figure this out? By analyzing the rocks' fractures and performing radiocarbon dating—a process usually used to tell the age of fossils—on charcoal that appears to have been buried by these ancient quakes.

SURVIVAL OF THE FITTEST

Surviving the destruction of a major earthquake can require pre-quake preparation and mental and physical strength. Oh, and plenty of luck.

Adalet Cetinol receives emergency treatment.

Turkey, August 1999

Yuksel Er was buried alive for more than four days under his home, which had been knocked down by an earthquake. How did he survive? "I told myself every morning that it was a new and beautiful day and wished myself luck for my struggle to come," he told reporters. But keeping a positive mental state was only half the struggle. Fighting off dehydration was not so easy. Yuksel did not have access to water, so he drank his own urine to stay alive.

Hope also helped Darcan Cetinol find his mother. Five days after a devastating earthquake struck his home, Darcan had a dream about his mother, who he believed died in the rubble. In his dream, he saw his mother, who was mute, calling out to him amid the ruins. This prompted Darcan to convince rescuers to find her. As he searched the rubble, Darcan heard humming noises, which he realized were coming from his mother. Rescuers carved out a hole big enough to pull 57-year-old Adalet Cetinol through. Perhaps the family's last name had something to do with her survival. Cetinol means "be tough" in Turkish.

Cinarcik, Turkey, August 1999

Four-year-old Ismail Cimen was playing with his toy truck when his life was changed forever. Two strong earthquakes struck, knocking down his home. When Ismail realized he was trapped under the balcony, he called for his parents. There was no answer. His mother was also trapped, and his father and sisters were dead. Ismail tried digging his way out of the rubble, but it was no use. He waited for 146 hours. His relatives had already prepared a grave for him. As his uncle searched for the family's bodies in the rubble, he shined his flashlight into an 18-inch (46-cm) opening. To his surprise, he saw his nephew peering up. Rescuers helped pull Ismail out of the wreckage. He suffered only from dehydration after six days without food or water. Fortunately for Ismail, kids need less water and space than adults, so they have a better chance of surviving under the rubble of a quake.

Ismail Cimen is held by a rescuer.

After more than five days of being stuck inside a building collapsed by a quake, two brothers, Sun Chi-kwang and Sun Chi-feng, were saved by rescuers. At the time of the quake, they had been playing card games. Even under the rubble, they had enough space to continue to play, which helped keep them in good spirits. While under the wreckage, the brothers celebrated Sun Chi-feng's birthday. "My older brother told me that never in my life did I celebrate his birthday with him, so I said today I would celebrate . . . and I gave him my necklace," Chi-kwang said. To keep their strength, the brothers ate rotten apples and drank what little water they had.

Workers pull Sun Chi-kwang out of the rubble.

Cracking Earthquake Construction

Why are some buildings reduced to a pile of rubble while others don't show a crack after a "big one" hits? For the past twenty-five years, scientists at the United States Geologic Survey have been studying Earth to figure out how to limit destruction caused by quakes.

Seismologists know that the ground directly above an earthquake's focus is the most sensitive area. They also know that soft ground, such as dirt and sand, shakes and breaks more violently than hard ground, such as rock. And they know that homes built with flexible materials, such as wood, can survive an earthquake better than homes built with harder materials, such as concrete.

How can tall structures, such as skyscrapers and bridges, stand up against shaky ground? Engineers have learned to make buildings move in sync with the ground instead of against it. A building's base needs to be shock-absorbing to withstand a quake. Many new buildings in quake-prone areas are built on a foundation of layers of steel and rubber, called base isolators, that absorb motion from the ground. Other buildings are fitted with a sliding surface so that the building won't rattle when the ground does.

Most older buildings were not built to survive a quake. For this reason, designers retrofit, or fix, older buildings and bridges with strong supports. After the 1989 Loma Prieta quake in California, scientists realized that the Golden Gate Bridge in San Francisco (left) was in danger of being destroyed by an earthquake with a magnitude greater than 7.0. They began retrofitting the bridge with base isolators, supports, and columns that would help the bridge move with and absorb strong tremors. Thanks to these techniques, the bridge can now withstand a quake as intense as 8.3.

Activity

PRE-QUAKE QUESTIONING Find out if your school is earthquake safe. Should it be? Imagine if a quake suddenly shook in the middle of the school day. Where would you go to be safe? What structures in different parts of the school create a safer environment? What might be a good idea to build or add to your school to make it quakeproof? What survival techniques might you use to keep yourself and others as safe as possible?

Rubble-Rousing Rescuers

When an earthquake hits, there's no time to lose. Every minute may mean pain, suffering, and even life or death to victims trapped in rubble. That's why only hours after the 1999 earthquake in Duzce, Turkey, a rescue team of firefighters, doctors, and engineers was on the scene. They had flown halfway around the world from Fairfax County, Virginia, to get there. The team's name: Virginia Task Force One, or VA-TF1. Their mission: finding and rescuing survivors.

No Time for Jet Lag

The seventy-member VA-TF1 is one of only two American search-and-rescue teams that can respond to emergencies in other countries. That's why they must move quickly, even though there's a lot to do even before they leave home. They must pack up everything they need—thousands of pounds of gear and equipment, including folding shower units, kerosene heaters, tents, medical supplies, computers, and radios—and make sure everything works. Then, they have to transport all of it to the airport.

Rescue flights abroad can be grueling and stressful, mainly because not all of the necessary site

information is available so soon after a disaster. The trip to Duzce involved almost twenty hours of flying through several time zones. But there's no time for jet lag. The team must be ready for action as soon as they land. In a foreign country, they never know what they'll find—or not find. "In international situations, most intersections do not have street signs," explains one team member. "Compound this with buildings collapsed into and blocking the streets and it becomes quite an ordeal."

After being briefed on the areas in which their help is needed, searchers pick their way through rubble and debris. They try to locate survivors with the help of small cameras, instruments that pick up faint sounds, and even specially trained dogs. Sometimes, no matter how hard they look, they get there too late.

But sometimes they get lucky. One team member recalls removing four live victims from the Izmit quake scene in ten hours—an exhausting but joyful day. Yet just when everyone thought the day's work was done, there was another surprise. Searchers found a forty-year-old man tightly entrapped with what they thought was another person. In mid-rescue, searchers realized the "other person" was actually the man's legs folded tightly against him.

To prepare for these situations, there's plenty of pre-site training. Team members must become skilled in specific types of rescue and learn things, such as how to tie knots strong enough to lift a car. But the most challenging practice is crawling through tight, dark spaces, like those they would find at an actual earthquake site. "We learn how to function without our eyes as much as we can and know our way around by touch and feel," notes Captain Jerry Roussillon, a team manager.

Risky Business

Even when an earthquake is over, the land and the people on it aren't safe. Aftershocks are common

The task force's truck is loaded on a cargo plane for a flight to the next mission.

Task force members check on a boy pulled from the rubble of a collapsed building in Turkey.

problems during search-and-rescue missions. Fortunately, the vibration-sensitive tools the team uses to locate survivors can also detect tremors. This helps them avoid being caught in a building during aftershocks. "Some aftershocks can register five on the Richter scale, which is significant and can cause more damage," says Roussillon. During a mission in the Philippines, the team located a man in a collapsed building. They began the difficult process of freeing him from the rubble, but they had to leave him several times because of aftershocks. The team finally got the man out alive, but only after nearly eight hours.

Aftershocks can be so hazardous that the team created a special rule for their base camp after their two experiences in Turkey: No supplies can be stacked more than waist high because of the danger of injury from items falling, and the team may start using Velcro™ to anchor laptop computers and telephones to shelves.

The members of VA-TF1 keep in shape through ongoing training programs at home. The most

challenging training topic is how to remove victims from rubble. The videos and photographs they use have their limitations. "You can show them the two-dimensional images, the destruction, and the dust, but it can't compare to the three-dimensional experience where you can actually taste the dust," says Roussillon, "or see a mother's tears."

Activity

READY, SET, GO! Imagine you've just been named the head of VA-TF1. The next morning, a quake hits downtown Tokyo, Japan. Considering that planes fly a polar route, estimate how many miles you'd have to travel to get from Fairfax, Virginia, to Tokyo. VA-TF1 uses the C-5 Galaxy U.S. Air Force transport plane. It is one of the world's largest aircraft, and its average speed is 541 miles (870 km) per hour. How long would it take you to get to Tokyo? How many hours do you think you'll need to get ready? Plan a schedule for your first two days of travel and work.

PLANNING AHEAD

Mayor Andrea Svalt stepped up to the podium and spoke into the cluster of microphones. "This is a very exciting moment," she said to the crowd of people and reporters at the Rolling Oaks town council meeting. "Ten months ago, we invited three young architects—all recent graduates from Rolling Oaks College—to design the new Rolling Oaks Public Library, complete with computer labs, high-speed Internet access, and specialized search engines linked to every major library in the country. Today, we will announce the winning architect and unveil plans for the new library!"

The crowd's cheers shook the meeting hall. Flashes lit up the room as reporters snapped dozens of pictures.

"I am proud to say," Mayor Svalt continued, "that all of the architects developed magnificent plans. I think any one of the designs would add to the architectural beauty of our city. But the final decision rests with our panel of judges, which is made up of our community's finest engineers. We mustn't forget that Rolling Oaks is situated very near a fault line, and we *must* make earthquake safety our top priority."

More applause from the crowd.

Mayor Svalt pointed to the V.I.P. section, where the engineers were seated. "Before our panel selects the best design, we've asked each architecture graduate to share their library plans with the members of the Rolling Oaks community."

Ted Topple approached the podium and unrolled the blueprint he developed. "I thought that the best way to ensure that our new library would be quake proof would be to create a foundation that could absorb the shock of a major earthquake," Ted said.

He pointed to the diagram of the building's base. "This structure would have alternate layers of steel

TED TOPPLE'S PLAN

Steel and rubber base on a hillside

plates and hard rubber sheets. The rubber would act like a sponge and absorb the shaking caused by a major earthquake. The steel plates would strengthen the foundation so that the weight of the building won't completely squash the rubber sheets. My proposed location is ideal: the hillside overlooking the Rolling River. There is easy access from the main roads and plenty of room for parking. Not to mention, of course, the beautiful view of the water below."

Ted took a small bow and rolled up the building plans as he returned to his seat.

Next, Roland Shaker took the stand. "I imagined the new library as the potential epicenter of Rolling Oaks, serving everyone in the community," he said. "Therefore, I've planned it on flat ground in the heart of the city. Our principal concern would be to use building materials that have a certain degree of flexibility—or ductility as we like to call it. We can reinforce all the concrete beams and columns with steel bars. I've also decided on a triangular pyramid-like design with a very stable base."

Finally, Jocelyn Quiverin unveiled her plan. "Our new library will be the strongest building in Rolling Oaks," she said matter-of-factly. "I envision making a building out of solid steel— one of the strongest building materials in the world. No amount of shaking, rattling, or rolling could possibly

ROLAND SHAKER'S PLAN

Pyramid design in the center of town

damage the structure. Furthermore, we would improve the quality of the Fillmore neighborhood by erecting the new library on the site of the old lake bed. The sandy ground should make digging easy, which of course will help keep the cost of the project down. Plus, the flexibility of the soil could absorb vibrations from an earthquake and act as a buffer to the entire building." Jocelyn thanked the audience and joined her fellow architects.

Mayor Svalt rose again and smiled at the library planners. "Thank you all for presenting your ideas. Remember, our team of engineers based their final decision on the best plan for sound construction and earthquake safety." At that point, the mayor motioned to her aide, who wheeled in a table from the adjacent room with a detailed model of the new library in its proposed location. "And here is the winning model!" Mayor Svalt exclaimed. "The groundbreaking ceremony begins tomorrow at noon!"

Can you figure out which model won and why? Use the clues below to help determine which building would continue to stand in an earthquake.

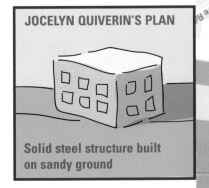

JOCELYN QUIVERIN'S PLAN

Solid steel structure built on sandy ground

Use these clues... Clues

1. Other natural disasters that can be caused by earthquakes include landslides, tidal waves, crumbled soil, and sand pits.

2. The quality of the soil can affect the stability of a building.

Answer on page 32

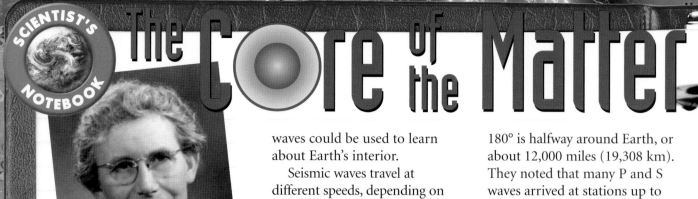

Copenhagen, Denmark, early 1930s

Inge Lehmann, Chief of the Seismology Department at the Royal Danish Geodetic Institute, looks closely at the seismograms of a powerful earthquake that shook New Zealand on June 16, 1929. The seismograms were recorded in three Soviet cities. They showed P waves arriving at the seismic stations about nineteen minutes after the earthquake.

Something wasn't right. These cities—7,300 to 9,200 miles (11,746 to 14,803 km) from the quake—shouldn't have felt P waves this strong. Like other seismologists, Lehmann knew that Earth was made of three layers—crust on the outside, a mantle beneath the crust, and a core in the center—and the waves had to flow through them. So what was wrong?

Flashback

In the early 1900s, seismologist Richard Dixon Oldham found that when an earthquake occurred, P and S waves showed up on seismograms all over the world. He realized that seismic waves could be used to learn about Earth's interior.

Seismic waves travel at different speeds, depending on the type of rock they're moving through. When the seismic energy hits a new layer of rock, some of it gets reflected back toward the surface, and some of it moves through the new layer at a different speed and direction. Oldham thought that if he could figure out where and how fast certain waves traveled, he could figure out how Earth was layered.

Oldham made an interesting observation: Waves traveling through the center of Earth arrived at seismic stations a few minutes later than they should have. He concluded that the waves must be slowing down somewhere in the middle of the planet. Oldham discovered Earth had a core made of different material than the other layers.

More Research Needed

As seismologists continued to study earthquake waves, they found more evidence for a core in the center of Earth. They found that P waves took longer than expected to appear because they were reflecting off the core.

Geologists soon noticed that P and S waves weren't registering on some seismometers. Seismologists speak of distances in terms of degrees, rather than miles or kilometers, away from the earthquake. For example, 180° is halfway around Earth, or about 12,000 miles (19,308 km). They noted that many P and S waves arrived at stations up to about 103° in any direction from the earthquake, and many P waves between 143° and 180° away. But there were no P waves between 103° and 143°.

The core was casting a "seismic shadow." When the P waves hit the core, some were changing direction in such a way that none came out in this area. Seismologists call this area the shadow zone (see diagram, right).

The other interesting thing seismologists noticed was that the S wave shadow zone was even larger than the P wave's. There were no S waves arriving past 103°. S waves didn't seem to be traveling through the core at all.

Seismologists knew that although P waves can travel through solids, liquids, and gases, S waves can only travel through solids. Because the P waves slowed down when they entered the core, and the S waves didn't seem to travel through the core at all, seismologists concluded that the core must be liquid.

Return to the 1930s

Inge Lehmann knew all of this when she studied the New Zealand earthquake seismograms and that is why she found them troubling.

First of all, they clearly showed P waves arriving in the shadow

An Inside Look at Earth

A "direct P wave" should move from the earthquake's focus through Earth to be felt on the other side (line **1**). But scientists found some P waves were reflecting off the outer core (line **2**). They also noted that P waves traveling through the solid inner core speed up (line **3**).

The shadow zone (between 103° and 143°) is the area on Earth in which P waves don't show up on seismographic data. This zone changes location depending on the site of an earthquake's focus. In the case of the New Zealand quake, the waves didn't register in the Russian cities of Irkutsk and Baku because they are located in the shadow zone.

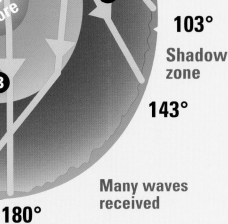

New Zealand earthquake focus 0°

outer core

liquid inner core

solid inner core

1 Many waves received

2

103° Shadow zone

143°

3

180° Many waves received

zone. Other seismologists had ignored these waves. They explained these as P waves that had reflected back and forth, bouncing around inside Earth until they got to the shadow zone. But surely, Inge thought, such a wave would lose its energy and be too weak to show up on seismograms in the shadow zone.

Secondly, some of the waves going through the core were arriving at stations sooner than expected. This suggested that something was speeding them up.

In 1936, Inge Lehmann came up with an explanation:

A hypothesis will here be suggested . . . although it cannot be proved from the data at hand. We take it that, as before, the earth consists of a core and a mantle, but that inside the core there is an inner core in which the [speed of the wave is greater] than in the outer core.

An inner core could explain the mysterious P waves arriving in the shadow zone. These waves had been reflected off the boundary between the outer and inner cores. An inner core could also explain the waves that were

traveling too quickly. They had been sped up when they entered the denser material.

Over the next forty years, seismologists were able to prove that Lehmann was correct. They also changed our understanding of the inner core. Using earthquake data, seismologists were able to determine its thickness (800 miles or 1,287 km) and show that unlike the outer core, the inner core is solid.

Activity

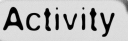

AROUND THE BEND Get a clear glass of water filled halfway with water and a straw. Dip the straw in the water and look at it from the side. What's happening at the point where the water meets the straw? According to the information on these pages, what might the straw represent in terms of an earthquake?

Terrific Temblor

Fire Starter

San Francisco's 1906 quake started a fire that swept across the city, made worse in part when the quake broke the city's major water main. Many people living outside of San Francisco at the time knew of the quake as the "1906 Fire" because local officials didn't want potential visitors or homeowners to be afraid of visiting the quake-prone city.

Quick Quake Quiz

Can you guess which . . .

❶ two states have the most earthquakes?

❷ state has the most damaging earthquakes?

❸ two states have the smallest number of earthquakes?

❹ continent has the fewest earthquakes?

Answers on page 32.

Kodiak Island, Alaska, 1964

Bears coming out of hibernation seemed to know a quake was coming. Usually they wake up and began searching for food, but that year they emerged two weeks earlier than usual and began leaving the area, which was soon the epicenter of a magnitude 8.4 quake.

Here are some other phenomena people claim to have seen before a big earthquake struck.

● On the southern coast of the Japanese island of Hokkaido, fish jumped into the air, landing on beaches and dying.

● In one Asian village, cats ran out of homes.

Shaky Stories

Long before scientists could explain what caused earthquakes, people created stories to explain them. The Japanese believed quakes were caused by a giant catfish called the *namazu*. This wiggly creature supposedly lived under the earth. In 350 B.C., Greek philosopher Aristotle claimed quakes were caused by the wind blowing through underground caves. The Roman poet Ovid said quakes happened because Earth got too close to the Sun, causing it to tremble from the big star's amazing radiance. Even in the 1800s, people were getting it wrong! A British scientist claimed waves were caused by underground water, which dripped on Earth's hot core, creating enough steam to shake the earth like a lid on a boiling pot.

Aristotle

Tidbits

Keep Your Eye on the Ball

Historians believe that Chinese philosopher Chang Heng invented the first "seismograph" in A.D. 132. Described as a large urn, it had eight dragon heads popping out of it. Each head faced one of the eight principal compass directions—North, South, East, West, Northeast, Southeast, Northwest, Southwest. A toad with its mouth open squatted below each dragon head. When an earthquake hit, a ball would release from one or more of the eight dragons and fall into that toad's mouth. Heng could tell the direction of the shaking by which ball was released. Some reports indicate that Heng's device detected an earthquake 400 miles (644 km) away; one that Heng and others near the ancient seismograph couldn't feel.

MIXED-UP MYTHS

Q: Can the ground open up during an earthquake and swallow people?

A: No. Only shallow cracks form during quakes. Faults do not open up during a quake.

Q: Will California ever break off and fall into the ocean?

A: No. However, Los Angeles is slowly creeping northward, so much so that it may someday end up next to San Francisco!

San Francisco, California, 1989

Baseball fans across the United States got quite a shock as they waited for Game 3 of the 1989 World Series to begin: A fifteen-second-long, 7.1 magnitude earthquake hit. The epicenter was located 65 miles (105 km) south of San Francisco's Candlestick Park, where the Oakland A's and the San Francisco Giants were set to play. Spectators at the stadium shook in their seats while TV viewers across the country saw their screens go fuzzy as announcers described events. The game was called off.

Time to Rock Most quakes only last a few seconds, but the biggest can last up to seven minutes. Aftershocks may continue for years.

WATER WEARY

An earthquake can shift large amounts of ocean water to create a huge tidal wave, called a tsunami. Tsunamis can be up to 50 feet (15 m) high, traveling up to 600 miles (965 km) an hour. One wave can build up enough speed to move more than 1,000 miles (1,609 km) across the sea to the shore. The California coast has been struck by tsunamis that began in Alaska and Japan.

So why can't we predict tsunamis and get out of their way? They travel so fast and hit without warning. To reduce the problem of tsunamis, the United States and Japan have set up tsunami warning stations, which sit 2.5 miles (4 km) out from the coastline and broadcast warning sirens if they detect one approaching.

Prove You're Quakeproof

Now that you know how destructive earthquakes can be, how people plan for and live through them, and how they can happen almost anywhere in the world, think about what you would do if one hit your neighborhood.

If your town is earthquake prone, it probably already has an earthquake disaster-assistance plan—though you probably don't know the details of it. Obviously, a real disaster-assistance plan for your town would take a team of professionals months, maybe even years, to construct. To get a taste of what that would be like, you and three classmates can produce an earthquake disaster plan for your city or town that includes the following:

1. A detailed list of where quakes might hit and do the most damage. This is something that emergency officials in your town could use. Do some research to see if there are faults running through your town and what they lie under. Which structures would be most likely to topple? What populations would be in the most danger? This paper could be very helpful for rescuers after a quake, so be specific and include all the information they would need to know.

2. A map of the area you are discussing with locations of important buildings and structures noted. Imagine that people were to find this map after a quake. Highlight what they'd need to know and be sure to include a map key.

3. A pamphlet to mail to residents on quake planning and safety measures that they can use in their homes. Remember, you don't want to cause mass panic, so be sure to phrase your writing simply and carefully.

4. A letter to mail to businesses, hospitals, care facilities, and schools. Think about how this information should differ from the pamphlet you would send to residents. Keep in mind that some of these buildings may be helpful in your planning.

5. Write a press release for local radio and television stations and online media. Remember that some people might not read your pamphlet, but they could get the information from the newspaper, TV, or Internet.

Present your project to the class and vote on who has created the best plan. It's important to be able to explain why that particular plan is best. Then contact your city council or fire department and request a copy of your community's existing disaster-assistance plan. What kinds of points does it include that you didn't know or think about?

ANSWERS
Solve-It-Yourself Mystery, pages 26–27:

Roland Shaker had the best design. A primary key in designing earthquake-resistant buildings is flexibility. An anti-seismic building should have some give and be able to sway without crumbling. The triangular design of the building is modeled after the Transamerica Building in San Francisco, California (right). The Transamerica Building is also built with steel-reinforced concrete columns and is twice as strong as the required building codes for the city. The building is also larger at its base, which significantly reduces the amount of sway during a massive temblor.

Ted Topple's design of steel plates layered with rubber sheets was also good as this protects a building by "padding" its foundation. Many buildings in Japan and California have these kinds of bases. The problem with Topple's plan wasn't in the building design, but in the proposed location: the hillside. Sometimes a hillside, especially one near water, could be prone to landslides, or the building could be shaken off its foundation and slip down the hill. The judges felt this plan could be risky.

Jocelyn Quiverin's plan suffered from bad structural design and poor location choice. Even though steel is very strong, it's not flexible and could crack under severe strain caused by a quake. Sandy lake beds, like landfills, are dangerous because the ground is usually weak, rocky, uneven, and permeated with water. During an earthquake, vibrations can cause liquefaction, which is when the particles in the ground loosen and the saturated soil begins to act like quicksand.

Fun & Fantastic Quiz, page 30:
1. Alaska and California, 2. California, 3. Florida and North Dakota, 4. Antarctica.

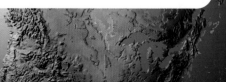